UNUSUAL PET PALS

PAT JACOBS

Crabtree Publishing Company

www.crabtreebooks.com

Crabtree Publishing Company
www.crabtreebooks.com
1-800-387-7650

Published in Canada
Crabtree Publishing
616 Welland Avenue
St. Catharines, ON
L2M 5V6

Published in the United States
Crabtree Publishing
PMB 59051
350 Fifth Ave, 59th Floor
New York, NY 10118

Published in 2019 by CRABTREE PUBLISHING COMPANY.

First published in 2019 by Wayland
Copyright © Hodder and Stoughton, 2019

Author: Pat Jacobs

Editors: Victoria Brooke, Petrice Custance

Project coordinator: Kathy Middleton

Cover and interior design: Dynamo

Proofreader: Melissa Boyce

Prepress technician: Samara Parent

Print and production coordinator: Katherine Berti

Photographs:
iStockphoto: Topaz777: p. 27 (top)
Shutterstock: p. 1, 5 (top right), 6–7 (bottom), 8 (bottom left),
12 (food and bottom left), 17 (top right), 23 (apple and carrots),
26, 27 (center right and bottom), 31
All other images courtesy of Getty Images iStock

Printed in the U.S.A./012019/CG20181123

Library and Archives Canada Cataloguing in Publication

Jacobs, Pat, author
        Unusual pet pals / Pat Jacobs.

(Pet pals)
Includes index.
Issued in print and electronic formats.
ISBN 978-0-7787-5730-6 (hardcover).--
ISBN 978-0-7787-5735-1 (softcover).--
ISBN 978-1-4271-2232-2 (HTML)

        1. Pets--Juvenile literature. 2. Pets--Behavior--Juvenile
literature. I. Title.

SF416.2.J33 2018   j636.088'7   C2018-905542-1
                                          C2018-905543-X

Library of Congress Cataloging-in-Publication Data

Names: Jacobs, Pat, author.
Title: Unusual pet pals / Pat Jacobs.
Description: New York, New York : Crabtree Publishing, 2019. |
  Series: Pet pals | Includes index.
Identifiers: LCCN 2018049843 (print) | LCCN 2018050494 (ebook) |
  ISBN 9781427122322 (Electronic) |
  ISBN 9780778757306 (hardcover : alk. paper) |
  ISBN 9780778757351 (paperback : alk. paper)
Subjects: LCSH: Pets--Juvenile literature.
Classification: LCC SF416.2 (ebook) | LCC SF416.2 .J33 2019 (print)
  | DDC 636.088/7--dc23
LC record available at https://lccn.loc.gov/2018049843

CONTENTS

UNUSUAL PETS

If you're looking for a pet pal with a difference, check out these cool creatures.

CHAMPION CHEWERS

Chinchillas and degus are South American **rodents**. These active animals need large, tall cages with plenty of space to jump and climb. Rodents' teeth never stop growing, so they have to chew to wear them down. Give these pets lots of chewing material in their cages, otherwise they may gnaw on the furniture when you let them out.

REMARKABLE REPTILES

Reptiles such as snakes and turtles are **cold-blooded** creatures, so they need to **bask** under a heat lamp to raise their body temperature. They also need an **ultraviolet (UV)** lamp to keep them healthy. Reptiles can carry a disease called salmonella, so it's very important to wash your hands after handling them.

AWESOME AMPHIBIANS

Amphibians start life in water, then grow legs and lungs. As adults, some live on land and others spend all or part of their time in water, but they all need damp conditions and dark hiding places. Amphibians have sensitive, delicate skin and should be handled as little as possible. Members of the salamander family, including axolotls and newts, can regrow lost limbs.

INTRIGUING INVERTEBRATES

Insects and spiders are **invertebrates**. Their bodies are protected by a tough outer shell, called an exoskeleton, that allows them to live in places where other creatures wouldn't survive. An insect's exoskeleton doesn't grow, so they have to shed it as they get bigger. Shedding, or molting, is a dangerous time in an insect's life, as their new exoskeleton is very delicate until it hardens.

TOP TIPS

- Never keep an animal that has been taken from the wild. It may have **parasites** and carry diseases, and it will not **adapt** well to life as a pet.

- Some of these animals have surprisingly long lifespans, so think about whether you'll be able to look after your pet for the rest of its natural life.

- It's best to keep your unusual pet pals in single-sex pairs or groups, or you may end up with many babies that you will need to find homes for.

- Never release an unwanted pet into the wild. Animals who have been pets rarely have the skills to survive and you could upset the balance of the natural environment.

- Consider adopting a pet. Having an older animal is a good solution if you're not sure you can care for it for 20 to 30 years.

CHINCHILLAS

Chinchillas are **nocturnal** animals, so they sleep during the day. They are active in the early mornings and evenings, and need to be let out of their cage at least once a day. They can live for more than 15 years.

TWO IS COMPANY

A single chinchilla will be lonely, so it will need at least one pal. It's best to choose same-sex littermates, or a **neutered** male and a female. If chinchillas don't already know each other, keep them side by side in separate cages until they get used to one another's scent. When you move them into the same cage, put their beds at opposite ends and give them separate dust baths (see page 7) until they're friends.

ROOM TO CLIMB

Chinchillas need a large cage with platforms to jump onto and branches to climb. They have very thick fur and can survive cold temperatures, but drafts are dangerous so keep them indoors. The cage should be away from heat vents and out of direct sunlight because they can easily overheat—if your pet's ears go red, it's too hot. Chinchillas need a hay-filled nest box that's big enough for them to cuddle up together, with an extra box so they can sleep alone if they want their own space.

TAMING AND EXERCISE

Before you let your chinchilla out of its cage, you'll need to **tame** it so you can catch it. Chinchillas love raisins, so train your pet to come to you for a raisin and then gently stroke it under the chin. Early evening is a good time to let your chinchilla out. Keep it confined to a small space and watch it carefully. Chinchillas love to explore and will chew anything—including electric cables, which is very dangerous!

FEEDING

Chinchillas need vitamin C, so chinchilla pellets are the best food for them. Good-quality hay provides fiber and wears down their teeth too. Don't give them too many treats—a rich diet can make chinchillas sick. They should always have fresh drinking water.

KEEPING CLEAN

Chinchillas clean their fur by bathing in fine dust, so you'll need a dust bath for your pet. You can buy chinchilla dust from pet stores, and it should be changed about once a week. Never use sand because it's too rough, and never put water on your chinchilla. If it gets wet, dry it with a towel immediately.

PET TALK

I love to play with cardboard boxes! Please put one or two in my cage. I'll probably chew them up, so make sure you take away any staples or plastic tape.

DEGUS

Degus make cute pets. They're active during the day, rarely bite, and love busy homes with lots of attention from their owners. They are social animals and should be kept in pairs or groups. They live for five to nine years.

Degus need a dust bath at least twice a week to keep their fur clean.

PET TALK

Please scoop me up from underneath my body. If you grab me from above, I'll think you're attacking me.

FEEDING

You can buy pellets for degus that provide everything they need to stay healthy. Sugar is very bad for them and they can easily get diabetes, so don't feed your pets fruit or sweet vegetables such as corn. They'll enjoy some leafy greens and should always have some good-quality hay in their cage to nibble on.

DEGU BEHAVIOR

Degus are social animals and communicate using noises such as tweets, chirps, whistles, and grunts. They come from Chile where they work together to build complicated burrows with nesting areas and food stores. Degus have ultraviolet vision—the white markings on their chest reflect ultraviolet light and show up when they stand on their hind legs to give an alarm signal.

HOME COMFORTS

These active animals need big cages with plenty of exercise space and different levels and ramps. If the cage has a wire-mesh floor, cover it with cardboard or hemp matting because it will damage your pets' feet. Degus love to dig and **burrow**, so they'll enjoy a box filled with potting compost or sand, and some clay-pipe tunnels. They can easily overheat, so they should be kept at a temperature below 68°F (20°C), and they hate wet or damp conditions.

GOOD TO KNOW

Degus have orange teeth. If their teeth turn white it's a sign they're not well. You should never catch your degu by its tail. It can shed the skin on its tail and run away. This is how they escape from **predators**.

CLEVER CREATURES

Degus are curious and intelligent—scientists were able to teach some how to use a rake to get food!—and they can be trained to use a litter box. Tree branches such as apple, pear, oak, beech, or ash will keep your pets busy and give them something to gnaw on, and they enjoy a treat ball or exercise wheel.

SNAKES

With regular handling and proper care, a snake can be a friendly and gentle pet. Many live for more than 20 years, so keeping a snake is a long-term commitment. Remember that you will need someone who is willing to look after your slithery pal if you go away.

SETTING UP A TANK

Snakes need an escape-proof tank that is long enough for them to stretch out fully. The width and height of the tank should be at least one third of your snake's length. Place a heat lamp over one side of the tank, where the temperature should be kept at 82.5 to 86°F (28 to 30°C). The cool side of the tank should be 68 to 75°F (20 to 24°C). Snakes also need an ultraviolet lamp. Snakes don't drink water, but they need a shallow bowl of water to soak in and to help keep the air in the tank moist.

FEEDING YOUR SNAKE

Snakes eat small animals, so you must be prepared to handle frozen baby mice, rats, or chicks. Never feed your snake live rodents because they might bite your pet. Make sure that a snake will accept dead **prey** before you buy it because some will only take live food. Snakes can open their jaws very wide and they swallow their prey whole. They normally only need to eat once a week, or once every two weeks.

PET TALK

Please make sure my food is completely defrosted before you feed it to me.

SKIN SHEDDING

Snakes shed their skins regularly. If your pet hides or stops eating, or if its skin looks dull and its eyes look cloudy, it may be about to shed. This is a stressful time for a snake. You can help by making sure it has a shallow dish of clean water to soak in, and put some smooth rocks or driftwood in the enclosure for your pet to rub against to loosen the skin.

BEST SNAKES FOR BEGINNERS

- Garter snakes are alert and active during the day. Females are about 3 feet (91 cm) long, while males are smaller. They live for up to 10 years.

- Corn snakes are easy to care for, but they are expert climbers and escape artists. They can grow up to 6 feet (183 cm) long and live for up to 20 years.

- Milk snakes are slow-moving snakes that grow up to 6 feet (183 cm) long and typically live for up to 20 years. They are nocturnal and should always be housed alone because one snake may eat the other.

- Ball pythons, also called royal pythons, grow up to 5 feet (152 cm) long and can live for up to 30, and even 50, years! They can be picky eaters, so make sure yours will eat dead prey before you take it home.

TURTLES

Turtles make great family pets, but they need a lot of space and care. Some turtles live for up to 30 years, and larger species may have to be moved to outdoor ponds when they are fully grown.

FEEDING

Offer your turtle a variety of foods, including raw meat and fish, live insects and worms, snails, berries, and leafy vegetables. Turtle pellets are also available. Turtles eat in the water and uneaten food drops to the bottom. This makes the water dirty, so many owners feed their pet in a separate water tank or bowl that's easy to clean.

TURTLE TANKS

Turtles need warm water to swim in, as well as a dry area where they can bask under a heat lamp. The tank should have 20 gallons (76 liters) of water per 2 inches (5 cm) of shell length. Your turtle should be able to swim without breaking the surface or touching the sides or bottom of the tank. Dirty water causes skin and shell problems, so get a powerful filter and clean the tank regularly. Turtles also need an ultraviolet lamp to stay healthy.

HIBERNATION

Wild turtles don't go into complete **hibernation** in the winter, but their heartbeats and breathing do slow down. This process is called brumation. If you're keeping your pet turtle warm with good lighting, it shouldn't feel the need to brumate.

BEST TURTLES FOR BEGINNERS

- Box turtles only grow up to about 6 inches (15 cm) long, so they are easy to handle. They love to bask under a heat lamp in the early morning and late afternoon.

- Painted turtles need lots of swimming space and prefer not to be handled. They can live for more than 30 years and grow up to 10 inches (25 cm) long.

- Map turtles have attractive markings and grow up to 10 inches (25 cm) long. They need clean water and plenty of oxygen, so it's worth adding an **airstone** to the water.

- Mud turtles spend more time on land than most other species. They rarely grow to more than 5 inches (13 cm) long, but they're not hands-on pets. They can be grumpy and sometimes bite.

- Diamondback terrapin turtles are active and curious pets that grow up to 8 inches (20 cm) long and need a large tank. In the wild, they live in **brackish** water, so it's a good idea to add a small amount of aquarium salt to their tank.

TAMING YOUR TURTLE

Turtles are naturally shy, so you need to gain their trust. Start by feeding your pet by hand. Once it comes over when you approach, try picking it up. Always handle your turtle gently and reward it with a treat afterward. Wash your hands thoroughly after touching your pet.

13

SALAMANDERS

Salamanders are nocturnal, but may adapt to being active during the day. Tiger and fire salamanders are most commonly kept as pets. They can live for more than 10 years, with fire salamanders sometimes reaching 30 years old.

CHOOSING YOUR PET

Make sure you buy a salamander that has been bred in **captivity**. Choose an adult, because young salamanders live underwater and need extra care. Fire and tiger salamanders can be kept in small groups in a large space, but males may fight over territory.

LIVING QUARTERS

Salamanders need a large, cool tank with a thick layer of moist potting soil or bark chips, and hiding places, such as a flowerpot turned on its side. A shallow dish of **chlorine**-free water will keep the tank damp and give your pet somewhere to bathe. They need a temperature between 65 to 70°F (18 to 21°C), so a cool room is the best place to keep them.

FEEDING

Salamanders like to eat crickets, earthworms, waxworms, and other bugs. Most prefer live food, but fire salamanders eat dead insects and chopped-up worms. Feed adults two to three times a week and remove uneaten food after 20 minutes. Never leave live bugs in the tank—they may injure your pet's skin!

TANK MAINTENANCE

Salamanders produce a lot of waste, and **bacteria** soon builds up in damp conditions, so you should spot clean the tank every day and wash it thoroughly with warm water and a scrubbing brush every week. Rinse it with chlorine-free water afterward. If **mold** appears in the tank, it is too damp.

HANDS OFF

Salamanders have delicate skin that can easily be injured. If you must pick up your pet, you should wash your hands in chlorine-free water and handle it with wet hands. Some species ooze **toxins**, so wash your hands immediately afterward.

AXOLOTLS

With their frilly **gills** and wide grins, axolotls make charming pets. A type of salamander also known as the Mexican walking fish, they are almost **extinct** in the wild but quite common as pets.

PET TALK

I'm very curious, so if you change the layout of my tank it will give me new places to explore.

SALAMANDERS THAT NEVER GROW UP

While most salamanders live in water as **larvae** but then move onto land, axolotls keep their cute baby features and spend their whole lives underwater. They typically live 15 years, with some reaching 20 years.

BOTTOM-DWELLERS

Axolotls are very active and live on the bottom of the tank. Sand is good to include in the tank but never use gravel as axolotls may swallow it. They usually grow to 10 inches (25 cm) long and need an aquarium that holds at least 10 gallons (37.9 liters) of water. Make sure your tank has a secure lid because axolotls have been known to climb out!

WATER QUALITY

Axolotl poop and food waste produces **ammonia**, so you need to grow friendly bacteria to get rid of it. A good water-testing kit from an aquarium store will explain how. The tank's water temperature should be 60 to 68°F (16 to 20°C). Clean the tank at least once a month, and change only 20 percent of the water every week, so you don't lose the healthy bacteria. Treat tap water with chlorine remover before adding it to the tank.

To move your axolotl, catch it in a soft net made of fine mesh that won't damage its fingers and gills.

FEEDING YOUR AXOLOTL

Axolotls should be fed once a day on brine shrimp, bloodworms, earthworms, or axolotl pellets. You can put the food in a bowl or a jar on its side, or feed your pet using tongs. Clear away any uneaten food or it will rot.

KEEP IT DARK

Axolotls have weak eyes and hate bright light, so if you have a tank light, turn it off as often as possible. Give your pet some dark hiding places, such as a plant pot turned on its side, or some aquarium ornaments.

NEWTS

Newts are active during the day and enjoy living in groups. They make interesting pets because they're always exploring, looking for food, and interacting with tank mates.

WHAT IS A NEWT?

A newt is a type of salamander. Chinese and Japanese fire-bellied newts are the types most commonly kept as pets. They are semiaquatic, meaning they spend time both on land and in water. They are happy at room temperature and may live for more than 15 years.

A PERFECT HOME

You will need a 10-gallon (37.9-liter) tank for up to four newts. A third of the tank should be a dry land area. You can add a piece of wood or make a mound of gravel to create a ramp for your newts to climb out of the water. Don't use small gravel pieces that your pets could swallow, or anything with sharp edges.

FEEDING

Newts enjoy bloodworms, crickets, earthworms, and maggots, but they can live happily on pellet food if you don't want to handle creepy-crawlies. You should feed your pets every other day and give them as much food as they will finish in 15 minutes. Remove any uneaten live food after 20 minutes. Some newts will take food from their owner's hand.

KEEP THE WATER CLEAN

Newts need about 10 inches (25 cm) of water at a temperature of 62 to 75°F (16.5 to 24°C), and it must be kept clean. If you have a filter, you should change 25 percent of the water every week, otherwise you'll need to change it every other day. A turkey baster is useful for this job because you can remove the dirtiest water from the bottom. Top it up with chlorine-free water at room temperature.

HANDLING YOUR PET

You should only handle your newt if it's absolutely necessary. Newts are very fragile and they ooze toxins from their skin to protect them from predators. If you must pick up your pet, wash your hands before and after, or wear clean plastic gloves.

FROGS

Pet frogs include **terrestrial** frogs that live on the ground, tree frogs, aquatic frogs that spend all of their lives in water, and semiaquatic frogs that live in water and on land.

FANTASTIC FROGS

Frogs are amazing creatures. They have excellent eyesight, with eyes that bulge out of their heads to allow them to see in almost every direction. They also never close their eyes—not even when they are sleeping! Some frogs can jump up to 20 times their body length in one leap. They also don't drink water because their skin **absorbs** it through a drinking patch on their belly.

FEEDING YOUR FROG

Frogs eat a variety of live insects, so if you're thinking of keeping frogs, you must be happy to handle the insects. Large frogs love to eat baby mice, but they shouldn't have too many because they're quite fatty.

CHOOSING A FROG

- **Aquatic frog**: African dwarf frogs are small and active. They spend their lives underwater, but they have lungs and breathe air, so they need a good amount of air space at the top of the tank. They do best when kept in groups, so plan to get at least three.

- **Semiaquatic frog**: Oriental fire-bellies are very active and easy to care for. Keep them in a tank with enough water so they can sit on the bottom with their eyes and nostrils above the water's surface. You can create a slope so they can leave the water, or float cork platforms on the water.

- **Tree frog**: White's tree frogs are good pets for first-time frog keepers. They need a tall tank with soil or bark on the bottom and branches they can climb. These frogs need a minimum temperature of 68°F (20°C) and **humidity** of 70 to 80 percent, which can be measured with a **hygrometer**. They should be fed live bugs two or three times a week.

- **Terrestrial frog**: Pacmans—named after the video game!—get quite large, but they aren't very active, so a 10-gallon (37.9-liter) tank is large enough for them. They need something to burrow into, such as coconut fiber or moss, and a shallow water bowl that they can sit in. They are nocturnal, and should have a temperature no lower than 65°F (18°C).

PET TALK

I like a change of scenery, so please rearrange the branches in my tank to keep me entertained.

21

MADAGASCAR HISSING COCKROACH

"Hissers" are one of the largest cockroach **species**. They come from the island of Madagascar off the African coast, where they often live in fallen logs. Unlike most cockroaches, they don't have wings.

GENTLE GIANTS

Madagascar hissing cockroaches grow up to 3 inches (7.5 cm) long and live for two to three years. They are easy and cheap to keep, and have a gentle nature. They hiss as a warning when they are upset, but males also hiss to attract a mate. Although cockroaches are associated with dirty places, hissers are very clean creatures and do not smell.

HISSER HOME COMFORTS

A 10-gallon (37.9-liter) tank is big enough for several hissers. Make sure it has a tight-fitting lid, because cockroaches can walk up glass and will soon escape if they can find any gaps. Your hissers will need somewhere to hide from the light, so add some cardboard tubes or egg cartons, or for a more natural look, make a tunnel out of tree bark.

HOT AND HUMID

Giant cockroaches come from tropical rain forests, so they are happiest at temperatures of 75 to 90°F (24 to 32°C). Spread damp potting soil over the base of their tank, and keep the enclosure moist at all times by spraying it with water. Cockroach tanks don't get very dirty, but they should be cleaned regularly because mold can grow, which causes allergies in humans.

FOOD AND DRINK

Hissing cockroaches enjoy fresh fruits and vegetables, especially carrots, apples, and bananas, and they also need food high in protein, such as dry dog or cat food. Remove any leftover food so it doesn't rot. Give your pets a little dish of water with a piece of sponge or cotton wool in it to stop them from drowning. They will also suck water droplets from the side of the cage when you spray it.

BABIES

It's easy to tell the difference between male and female hissers, as males have horns at the back of their head. Unless you have homes for large numbers of baby cockroaches, you should get two males. If you have a mixed-sex pair, or if your female cockroach was in contact with a male before you brought her home, you could end up with 20 to 60 babies!

STICK INSECTS AND MANTISES

Stick insects and praying mantises have different diets, but they need similar homes. A tank or even a large, tall glass jar will be suitable for either pet. You should spray their enclosure with water every few days, so they can drink water droplets off the leaves.

A TALL ENCLOSURE

Stick insects and mantises shed their exoskeletons, or shells, by clinging to a branch and stepping out of the old one. They need an enclosure that's at least three times as tall as a fully grown adult insect. If they don't have space to slide out of their old exoskeleton, they may get stuck and die. The floor should be covered with a kitchen towel for easy cleaning and the top should have **ventilation** holes, or be covered with netting, so your pets receive enough fresh air.

A LEAFY DIET

Stick insects need fresh leaves and branches at all times. Place branches in a jar of water. Leaves that are safe for your pets are privet, rose, oak, hazel, and bramble (but older leaves only, not the pale-green new growth). Make sure they haven't been sprayed with insect or weed killer.

BABIES

Female stick insects can produce young without a mate. If you see eggs at the bottom of the enclosure it's best to remove them, or you'll have a population explosion.

PRAYING MANTIS ENCLOSURE

Praying mantises like to sit up high, so fill their enclosure with branches or artificial plants that they can climb on. The base should be covered in a material that can be kept damp, such as a kitchen towel, potting soil, shredded bark, or sand, so the enclosure stays humid. Mantises come from warm parts of the world, so your pet may need a small heating pad in the winter.

AN INSECT DIET

Mantises are ambush predators, meaning they lie in wait, ready to pounce on their insect prey. If you're not happy feeding them live insects, a praying mantis isn't for you. An adult mantis will eat one or two crickets or flies a day, and uneaten prey should be removed after one hour.

MOLTING

A mantis will stop eating a day or two before it sheds its exoskeleton. It's especially important to remove any uneaten food from the enclosure at this time because a freshly molted mantis could be injured by its prey. Don't feed your mantis for 24 hours following its molt and never try to pick it up during this time.

PET TALK

I grow wings when I'm an adult, so I might fly away if you let me out.

25

TARANTULAS

Tarantulas make fascinating pets. There are two types of tarantulas: terrestrial, which live on the ground and like to burrow, and arboreal, which live in trees. For your first tarantula pal, a terrestrial one is recommended as they are easier to care for.

HOUSING

Tarantulas are not social creatures, so your pet should have its enclosure to itself. A 5-gallon (19 liter) tank is best. On the floor of the tank, add 2 to 4 inches (5 to 10 cm) of potting soil for your spider to burrow into. Your pet will also want a place to hide, such as a hollow log or a flowerpot turned on its side. Tarantulas don't like bright lights, so keep the tank away from direct sunlight. The temperature in the tank should be 75 to 85°F (24 to 29°C). Heating pads to warm the tank can be purchased at many pet stores.

FEEDING

Adult tarantulas only need to eat once or twice a week. Their main diet is live crickets, but you can feed them worms or roaches once in a while. A large part of caring for a tarantula is also caring for the live crickets they will eat. Crickets should be coated with vitamin powder before being fed to your spider pal.

HEALTH TIPS

If the humidity level in your pet's tank is not high enough, it can become sick. You can measure the humidity level with a hygrometer. Depending on what species of tarantula you have, you will need to mist your pet with water either once a week or more frequently. A shallow dish of water should also be kept in the tank.

PET TALK

Please place a few small rocks in my water dish so I have something to climb on, otherwise I may drown.

LOOK, BUT DON'T TOUCH

You should think of your pet tarantula like a fish— it is for observing only. Some people do handle their tarantulas, but this is not recommended. Tarantulas do bite, and their bites contain poison, although the amount of poison is typically similar to a bee sting. But just as a bee sting can seriously harm humans, so can tarantula bites.

UNUSUAL PETS QUIZ

How much do you know about your unusual pet pals? Take this quiz to find out.

1 **What sort of animals are chinchillas and degus?**

    a. Reptiles
    b. Rodents
    c. Amphibians

2 **How do you know if a chinchilla is too hot?**

    a. It starts to sweat
    b. It lies on its back
    c. Its ears go red

3 **When are degus most active?**

    a. During the day
    b. At dawn and dusk
    c. At night

4 **How long should a snake's tank be?**

    a. A third of its adult length
    b. Its full adult length
    c. Twice its adult length

5 **How are axolotls different from most salamanders?**

    a. They spend their whole lives on land
    b. They are vegetarians
    c. They spend their whole lives underwater

6 Why should you avoid handling your newts if possible?

a. They have very fragile skin
b. Their skin produces toxins
c. Both of these

7 What sort of frog is an oriental fire-belly?

a. Terrestrial
b. Semiaquatic
c. Tree

8 How do you tell male and female hissing cockroaches apart?

a. Males have wings
b. Females are lighter in color
c. Males have large horns at the back of their head

9 Why do stick insects and praying mantises need a tall enclosure?

a. They need a lot of exercise
b. So they have room to step out of their old exoskeleton
c. So they have room to jump

10 How often do adult tarantulas need to eat?

a. Every four hours
b. Once or twice a week
c. Once a day

QUIZ ANSWERS

1 What sort of animals are chinchillas and degus?

    b. Rodents

2 How do you know if a chinchilla is too hot?

    c. Its ears go red

3 When are degus most active?

    a. During the day

4 How long should a snake's tank be?

    b. Its full adult length

5 How are axolotls different from most salamanders?

    c. They spend their whole lives underwater

6 Why should you avoid handling your newts if possible?

    c. Both of these

7 What sort of frog is an oriental fire-belly?

    b. Semiaquatic

8 How do you tell male and female hissing cockroaches apart?

    c. Males have large horns at the back of their head

9 Why do stick insects and praying mantises need a tall enclosure?

    b. So they have room to step out of their old exoskeleton

10 How often do adult tarantulas need to eat?

    b. Once or twice a week

LEARNING MORE

BOOKS

Crossingham, John and Bobbie Kalman. *The Life Cycle of a Snake*.
Crabtree Publishing, 2003.

Houser, Grace. *Chinchillas (Our Weird Pets)*. PowerKids Press, 2017.

Silverstein, Dr. Alvin and Dr. Virginia Silverstein and Laura Silverstein Nunn.
Hissing Cockroaches: Cool Pets! Enslow Elementary, 2011.

WEBSITES

https://kids.nationalgeographic.com/explore/nature/super-snakes
Visit this site for tons of information, pictures, games, and videos about snakes.

www.kidcyber.com.au/axolotls
This website has information and videos about axolotls.

GLOSSARY

absorb To take in or soak up

adapt To become used to new conditions

airstone A piece of equipment that increases water circulation and oxygen in the water

ammonia A stong-smelling chemical that is harmful to animals

amphibians Animals that start life underwater as larvae with gills. As adults, most grow lungs, breathe air, and live on land.

bacteria Microscopic living things that are found everywhere

bask To lie in sunlight or under a heat lamp to warm up

brackish Slightly salty water, a mix of seawater and river water

burrow To dig a hole or tunnel to hide in

captivity To be confined in an area, not free to roam

chlorine A chemical in tap water that kills bacteria

cold-blooded Animals whose body temperature changes according to their surroundings

extinct No longer in existence

gills Organs on the side of the head that act like lungs and absorb oxygen from water

hibernation To sleep during winter

humidity The amount of moisture in the air

hygrometer An instrument that measures humidity

invertebrates Animals without a backbone

larvae Newly hatched form of a fish, amphibian, or insect

mold A type of fungus

neutered An animal that has had an operation to stop it from making babies

nocturnal An animal that sleeps during the day and is active at night

parasite An animal that lives in or on another creature and feeds from it

predator An animal that hunts and eats other creatures

prey An animal that is hunted by other animals

reptiles Animals with scaly skin that crawl on their bellies

rodents Animals that gnaw and have constantly growing incisor teeth

species A group of closely related organisms

tame To train a living thing to be friendly and gentle

terrestrial An animal that lives on the ground

toxins Poisonous substances

ultraviolet (UV) The part of sunlight that is invisible to humans but visible to some living creatures

ventilation Allowing for proper airflow

INDEX

Oh, the Things We're FOR !

By
Innosanto Nagara

TRIANGLE SQUARE
books for young readers

7 SEVEN STORIES

New York • Oakland • Liverpool

When you go to a march
and raise your sign high,
you'll make people smile
who thought you were shy.

And you'll make people wonder,
does that kid *really* know why?

You DO know of course,
that's why you are there.
You're there to say NO!   Because you DO care.
You're there to say STOP!   What's happening's not fair.

We can't keep doing what we're doing the way it's been done.
We can't keep using it, moving it, running it how it's been run.
Standing together! That's how change can be won.

So yes.
You DO know what's up, and why you are there.

But that's NOT the Big Question.
At least not for me.
It's not folks who don't know
or just disagree.
It's folks who *want* to be with us
but *feel* that they just,
that they simply just
can't
see.

Folks who say,
We want to RESIST!
We're on the same page.
Our problems are serious,
that's easy to see.
Destruction must stop,
we can't let it be.

Stop polluting! And poisoning!
And cheating and stealing!
No one likes dictators
or violence
or kids going hungry.
End poverty! Stop war!
But okay,
then what are you *for*?

NO MORE
DEATHS

STOP

NO DRILLING
NUKES

END THE
VIOLENCE

NO
JUSTICE
NO
PEACE

STRIKE

OUT OF THE
MIDDLE EAST

NEVER
AGAIN

STOP
CLIMATE
CHANGE

BA
TH
BO

NU
BLOOD
FOR OIL

Oh, what are we for!

That
Is my favorite question.

And I'm sure it's yours too,
because *you* pay attention.

You have so many answers.
And so many options.
And so many *solutions* that you want to impart.
The only hard question is where does one start?

BREAK THE SILENCE

NO BAN NO WALL

END APARTHEID

BOYCOTT

STOP THE PIPELINE

NO WAR

END THE OCCUPATION

SHUT IT DOWN

RESIST

STOP BUILDING PRISONS

NO KIDS IN CAGES

END the SANCTIONS

We have to start somewhere, so let's take a pick.
Take something we all do: we ALL get sick.

We get wheezy and sneezy and snuffly noses.
We get headaches and tummy-aches and sometimes throw up.

So we sip some hot soup and we get a good rest,
and soon we feel better and back to our best.

But sometimes being sick is harder than that.

The nurses may say we need more than just rest.
The doctors may want to give us a test.
Perhaps they'll tell us to get an X-ray.
It might even mean a hospital stay.

And when there's a virus that starts to run wild,
more people get sicker (though some cases are mild).
But so many sickies means so many meds
and not enough nurses and not enough beds.

But THEN
we are asked,
who's gonna PAY?

Sadly the answer
       is pretty not funny.
When companies decide
       to make all their money
deciding WHO gets cared for
       and who does not,
depending on cash
       you put in their pot.

So IF you have means,
   you get care that you need.

But if you don't . . . well . . .
   you're in trouble indeed.

So here's an idea that we can ALL share:
We ALL do our part and put in what's fair.
And then when we need it,
we have access to care!

So Health Care for ALL
is a thing that we're for.
Should I go on?
Continue this tour?

No problem.
For sure.

HEALTH CARE FOR ALL

We all know now
that the climate's a-changin'.
The earth is a- warmin', and the sea levels risin'.
The ice shelves are melting
which is not all surprising,

since SCIENCE was warning
that the globe will keep warming
if we keep burning the stuff we've been burning.

But IS there an answer?
Some people may ask.

Why YES! you say.
If we're up to the task.

Look up! you exclaim.
What do you see?
A HUGE ball of plasma!
Clean energy for free!

So instead of drilling and spilling and (let's be honest) even killing
for dirty dead dino goop that should stay in the ground,
let's embrace the sun, and wind, and earth . . .
Nature's power will always abound.

If anyone's STILL not sure what you mean,
what we can change so our future is GREEN,
well, it starts with committing to making it real,
working together to seal a NEW DEAL!

Wow, they say.
Universal Health Care? they say.
Solar energy?
Such big things for a kid.

Okay. That's cool.
But shouldn't you be focused on kid things?
Like playdates? And school?

School and play!
Why yes! On that, you have MUCH to say!
We learn more with more recess
and time to eat lunch.
Much smaller classes.
We can't learn in a crunch.

If we memorize and drill
and are taught to be tested,
real thinking does not get invested.
Critical minds can't flourish that way.

And speaking of teaching,
our teachers need
MUCH better pay!

We need schools that are safe.
We need freedom to range.
We need libraries and sports.
We need cultural exchange.

THEATER
SPORTS
ART
MUSIC

We need music and arts
to fill our brains and our hearts.
We should be seen as WHOLE people
with many DIFFERENT kinds of smarts.

There are so MANY ideas upon which we can call.
For a free and fair (and PUBLIC) education for all!

DANCE

WELLNESS

But let's get more personal.
Let's talk about WE.
Let's talk about YOU.
Let's talk about ME.
Let's talk about US.
And the many many
        ways we can BE.

Let's celebrate the splendor
of spectrums of gender.

Let's recognize and value
  the many hues of our skin.
The many languages we speak.
  Our many lands of origin.

To whom one may pray.
  With whom one shares love.
The diverse ways our minds work.
  Our bodies, we're proud of.

Those who've always been here
  on whose lands we now tread.
Those who dare speak up.
  Those who act quietly instead.

But let's also be clear that harm has been done.
Futures were stolen by sword and by gun.

We can't flip a switch
   and say that we're there.
A history of injustice
      takes more to repair.
To balance the scales
   we must reclaim what they stole.
And do the hard work
to make us ALL whole.

Making us whole.
That's really the theme.
It's not as difficult as it may seem.

Lock them up! they say.
Throw away the key!
That's the quick fix that some want to see.

But let's take a moment and take a close look.
Who gets locked up? Where, how, and why?
You'll see there's a problem that one can't deny.
A pattern of how the judgments we face
are different for each based on money and race.

And even IF things
    were (quote unquote) fair,
        and those doing time (quote unquote) deserve to be there,
        is putting humans in cages the best we can do?
        In 10,000 years have we learned nothing new?

            We have, of course,
            and that's the good news.
            There are much better options
            from which we can choose.

    Lift up the idea that we dispose of no one.
    We're each of us MORE than our worst, worst act.
    There's no panacea and WORK must be done.
    Liberation's for all of us. Or else it's for none.

Speaking of WORK, we've ideas there too.
Things we can change, things we can do.

So many people work hard-hard for their pay.
But hardly make ends meet at the end of the day.

And as if just working wasn't hard-hard enough,
they're all alone when the going gets rough.
There are SO many ways that these things can be tough.
We don't even have room to list ALL of that stuff.

But suffice it to say, there's many a way
where workers have rights and workers have sway.
Where we work with each other in Union as one.
Or better yet, in co-ops, for fairness (and fun)!

And when our rights come under attack,
we will know who's got our back!

Okay. I know. This is a lot.
But hey, they asked, so they get what you got.

They opened the door for solutions galore
when they asked you, What are you for?

Maybe they'd hoped
for something lighthearted.
But you, my friend,
are just getting started.

So as you can see, there's much to be done.
Much to be fixed and much to be run.

But having to DO stuff isn't so bad.
Let's roll up our sleeves! Let's do something rad!

Let's SHOUT OUT solutions from sea to sea!
Let's yell out our favorites!
(I hope you'll join me.)

FAIR TRADE

PUBLIC

SPHERE RESERVES

OPEN SOURCE

DISABILITY ACCESS

AFFORDABLE

WORKER-OWNERSHIP

GOOD JOBS!

WILDLIFE PROTEC

PAID FAMILY LEAVE!

PUBLIC SPACE!

MICROCREDIT!

SCIENCE!

THE COMMO

CHOICE

PARTICIPATORY ECO

LOCAL CURRENCY!

TEACHING NO

WALKABLE CITIES

RECLAIM THE STREETS! EQUAL

PUBLIC EDUCATION!

SEX EDUCATION

MUTUAL AID! PROJEC

UMAN R

FEED TH

GRAYWATER!

PECT THE TREATIES!

FREE RAN

IBRARIES! FREE BUS!

MICROGRIDS

HOMES FOR ALL!

CULTURALLY RESPONSIV

PUBLICLY FUNDED ELECTIO

REPRODUCTIVE FREEDOM! DUAL-IMMERSI

WORKERS' RIGHT

COLLECTIVE BARGAINING

To YOU these ideas are never a bore.
You've already shared many,
and have many, many, many, oh, so, so many, many more!

When you care for the world as much as you do,
   creating solutions is oh, so, so you.

        Of course not ALL solutions are the best they can be.
            And on some things, we may disagree.

        But it all starts with caring,
                and agreeing to sharing.
        A radical act, if we are daring.

But this is all stuff that YOU already know.

YOU'RE ready to go. You're ready to soar.
You're ready to start. You're ready to ROAR!

So off now let's go!
Let us start working.
Let us start building
the future we're FOR!

SOME THINGS THAT I'M FOR:

DEDICATED TO ARIEF ROMERO
AND HIS MAMA, KRISTI

Thank you as always to all the kids and their families who read and listened to my drafts and gave me your feedback. You are redefining who gets to decide what makes a children's book a children's book.

It takes a community for a book to come to life and I have so many people to thank. Thank you Kristi for always supporting me. Thank you, my Orchard communty for creating the space—particularly my housemates, who had to endure my takeover of the living room to finish this book. Thank you, my Bay Area children's book community (Fight Club!), for making this a Movement. Thank you, Dan Simon, for your trust in me, and patience. Thank you, Ruth Weiner and the rest of the crew at Seven Stories Press/Triangle Square Books for Young Readers for all that you do to get these works in front of kids.

ABOUT THE AUTHOR

Children's book author and illustrator **INNOSANTO NAGARA**'s books encourage children to grow up with confidence in themselves, their rights, and the agency they have to shape their future.

Born and raised in Indonesia, Inno moved to the US to study zoology and philosophy at UC Davis. He then moved to the San Francisco Bay Area, working as a graphic designer for a range of social change organizations before founding the Design Action worker-owned cooperative design studio in Oakland, California. Inno lives in a cohousing community with nine adults and eight children, and teaches and trains martial arts at a collectively run dojo. Basically, he is all about building the democratic society we want to see, today.

Inno's first book, *A is for Activist*, is credited with starting the movement in social justice book publishing for children. After that came *Counting on Community, My Night in the Planetarium, The Wedding Portrait*, and *M is for Movement*. *Oh, the Things We're For!* is Inno's sixth book.

Seven Stories Press
140 Watts Street
New York, NY 10013
www.sevenstories.com

ISBN 978-1-64421-014-7 (hardcover)
ISBN 978-1-64421-015-4 (ebook)

Library of Congress Cataloging-in-Publication Data has been applied for.

Printed in China.